Song of
Creation

©2004 Paul Goble

Published 2004 by Eerdmans Books for Young Readers
An imprint of Wm. B. Eerdmans Publishing Company
255 Jefferson S.E., Grand Rapids, Michigan 49503
P.O. Box 163, Cambridge CB3 9PU U.K.

Printed and bound in China
04 05 06 07 08 09 10 7 6 5 4 3 2 1
ISBN 0-8028-5271-8
A catalog record of this book is available from the Library of Congress

Note

In the Book of Daniel (The Prayer of Azariah and the Song of the Three Young Men), this song in praise of God saved the three young men from death in the furnace, reminding us of the power of prayer. Many people will know the song from *The Liturgy of the Hours*, others from *The Book of Common Prayer*, which is where I first came upon it when at St. Edward's School in Oxford, England.

In this children's book form, it seemed necessary to make some changes in verse order to fit comfortably with the illustrations, and a few words and verses were changed or left out. I hope no harm has been done to the spirit of the original. It is illustrated with the American scene because the canticle's praises are relevant to our gardens and parks anywhere. A few verses have been added in small type, to encourage readers to add many more verses of their own.

Paul Goble, Black Hills, South Dakota

I hope that this book will help to open people's eyes to see God's presence all around them. The words of the Benedicite should be a launch-pad for people to sing their own praise to God, helping them to recognize God's hand just as much in the song of a bird as in the growth of a thistle. When we think we are alone, fighting the forces of darkness, think again. If you are fighting for God, then his angels will be fighting for you. We live in a world that hates suffering and seems to think that all bad things point to the absence of God. This song points in the other direction: if in the heat of adversity we can praise God, he will deliver us.

Rev'd Dr. Andrew Bunch,
The United Benefice of Oxford St. Giles, St. Philip and St. James
with St. Margaret, Oxford, England

The illustrations were rendered in watercolor.
The type was set in Caslon.
Graphic Design Matthew Van Zomeren

Song of
Creation

By Paul Goble

Eerdmans Books for Young Readers
Grand Rapids, Michigan • Cambridge, U.K.

O you meadowlarks, bless you the Lord:
praise him, and magnify him forever.

O all my ancestors, bless you the Lord:
praise him, and magnify him forever.

O my family, bless you the Lord:
praise him, and magnify him forever.

O all my descendants, bless you the Lord:
praise him, and magnify him forever.

O you magpies, bless you the Lord:
praise him, and magnify him forever.

O all you works of the Lord, bless you the Lord:
praise him, and magnify him forever.

O you dandelions, bless you the Lord:
praise him, and magnify him forever.

O you hawks, bless you the Lord:
praise him, and magnify him forever.

O you cranes, bless you the Lord:
praise him, and magnify him forever.

O you heavens, bless you the Lord:
praise him, and magnify him forever.

O you nighthawks, bless you the Lord:
praise him, and magnify him forever.

O you angel messengers of God, bless you the Lord:
praise him, and magnify him forever.

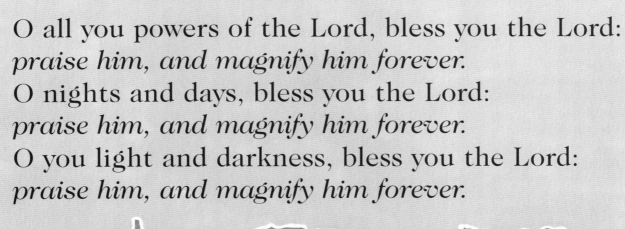

O all you powers of the Lord, bless you the Lord:
praise him, and magnify him forever.
O nights and days, bless you the Lord:
praise him, and magnify him forever.
O you light and darkness, bless you the Lord:
praise him, and magnify him forever.

O you sun, bless you the Lord:
praise him, and magnify him forever.
O you fire and heat, bless you the Lord:
praise him, and magnify him forever.

O you vultures, bless you the Lord:
praise him, and magnify him forever.

O you moon, bless you the Lord:
praise him, and magnify him forever.
O you stars of heaven, bless you the Lord:
praise him, and magnify him forever.

O you moths, bless you the Lord:
praise him, and magnify him forever.

O you frost and cold, bless you the Lord:
praise him, and magnify him forever.
O you ice and snow, bless you the Lord:
praise him, and magnify him forever.

O you redpolls, bless you the Lord:
praise him, and magnify him forever.

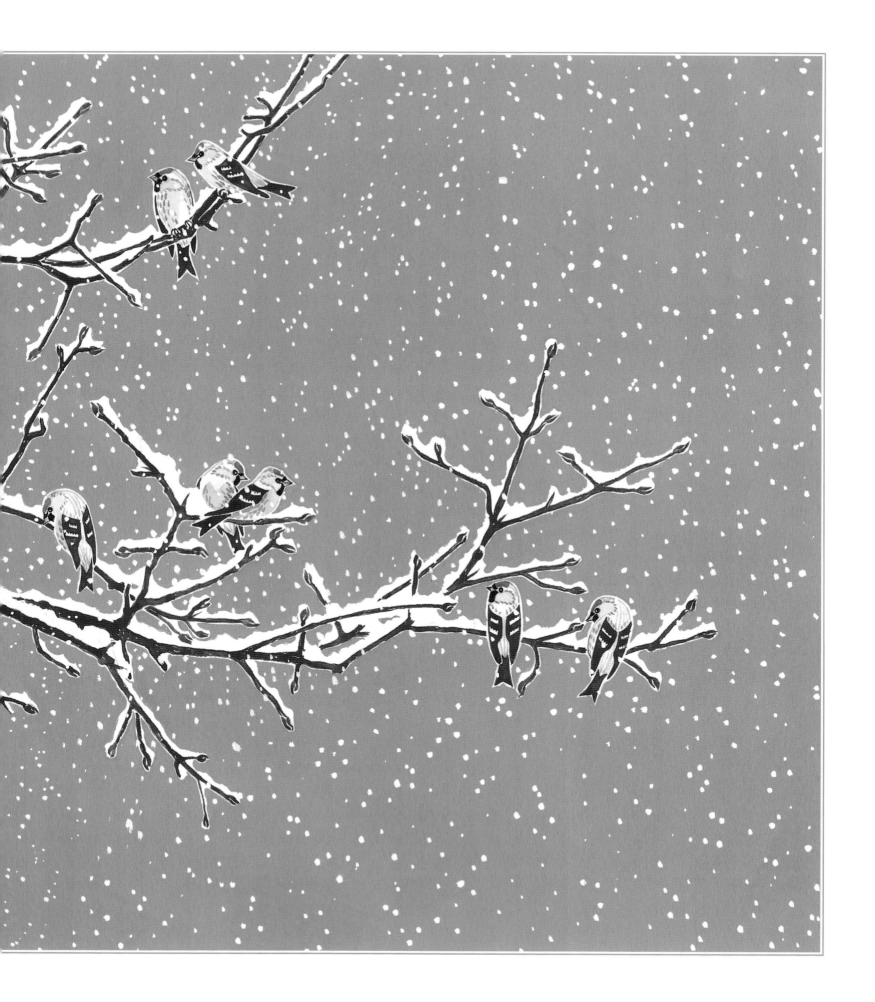

O you waters above the heavens, bless you the Lord:
praise him, and magnify him forever.
O you showers and dew, bless you the Lord:
praise him, and magnify him forever.

O you irises, bless you the Lord:
praise him, and magnify him forever.

O you winds of God, bless you the Lord:
praise him, and magnify him forever.
O you lightnings and clouds, bless you the Lord:
praise him, and magnify him forever.

O you moose, bless you the Lord:
praise him, and magnify him forever.

O you geese, bless you the Lord:
praise him, and magnify him forever.

O you eagles, bless you the Lord:
praise him, and magnify him forever.

O you ravens, bless you the Lord:
praise him, and magnify him forever.

O let the earth bless the Lord:
yes, let it praise him, and magnify him forever.
O you mountains and hills, bless you the Lord:
praise him, and magnify him forever.

O you elk, bless you the Lord:
praise him, and magnify him forever.

O you forests, bless you the Lord:
praise him, and magnify him forever.

O you green things of the earth, bless you the Lord:
praise him, and magnify him forever.

O you pine trees, bless you the Lord:
praise him, and magnify him forever.

O you horses, bless you the Lord:
praise him, and magnify him forever.

O you springs of water, bless you the Lord:
praise him, and magnify him forever.
O you lakes and rivers, bless you the Lord:
praise him, and magnify him forever.

O you avocets, bless you the Lord:
praise him, and magnify him forever.

O you gulls, bless you the Lord:
praise him, and magnify him forever.

O you cormorants, bless you the Lord:
praise him, and magnify him forever.

O you bass and trout, bless you the Lord:
praise him, and magnify him forever.

O you fishes and all that move in the waters,
bless you the Lord:
praise him, and magnify him forever.

O you sunfishes, bless you the Lord:
praise him, and magnify him forever.

O you sturgeon, bless you the Lord:
praise him, and magnify him forever.

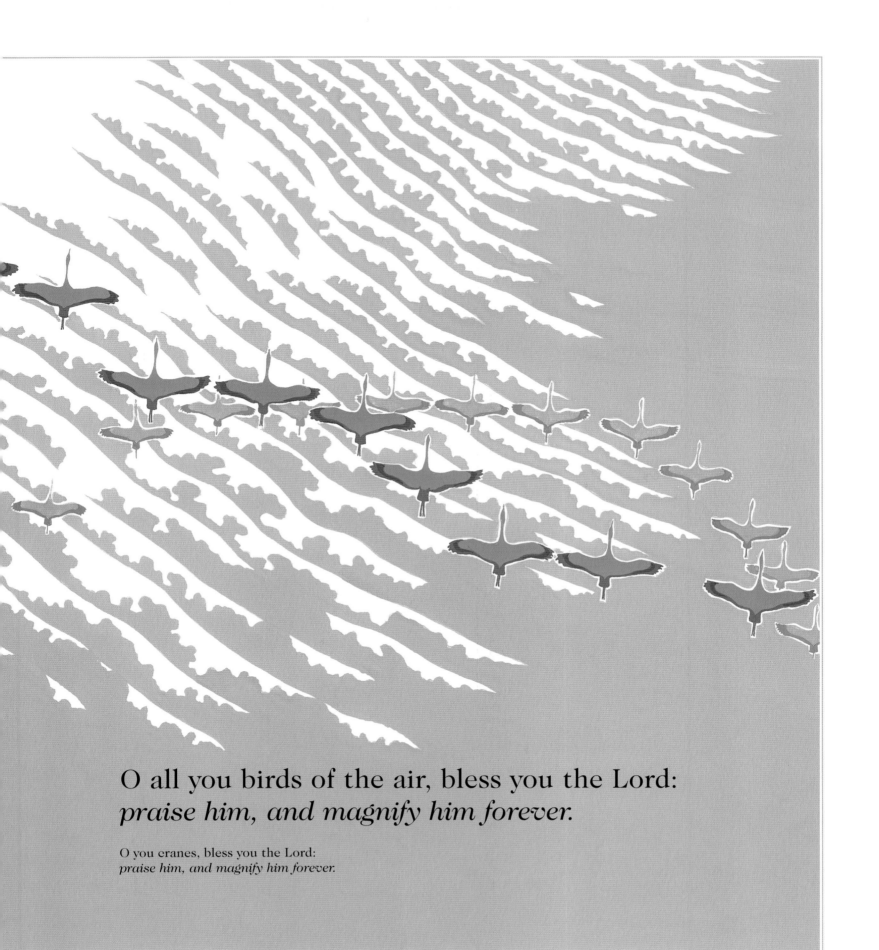

O all you birds of the air, bless you the Lord:
praise him, and magnify him forever.

O you cranes, bless you the Lord:
praise him, and magnify him forever.

O you buffalo, bless you the Lord:
praise him, and magnify him forever.

O you wolves, bless you the Lord:
praise him, and magnify him forever.

O you crows, bless you the Lord:
praise him, and magnify him forever.

O all you animals, bless you the Lord:
praise him, and magnify him forever.

O let all people bless the Lord:
yes, let them praise him, and magnify him forever.
O you children, bless you the Lord:
praise him, and magnify him forever.
O you holy and humble of heart, bless you the Lord:
praise him, and magnify him forever.
O all you spirits and souls, bless you the Lord:
praise him, and magnify him forever.
O give thanks to God, because he is good:
because his mercy endures forever and ever.
Amen.